Start Your Day With Hope

Wayne Beaton

TEACH Services, Inc.
P U B L I S H I N G
www.TEACHServices.com

Copyright © 2013 and TEACH Services, Inc.
ISBN-13: 978-1-57258-933-9 (Paperback)
ISBN-13: 978-1-57258-934-6 (ePub)
ISBN-13: 978-1-57258-935-3 (Kindle/Mobi)

Library of Congress Control Number: 2012950842

Unless otherwise noted, all scripture is taken from the King James Version Bible.

Published by

TEACH Services, Inc.

P U B L I S H I N G

www.TEACHServices.com

Table of Contents

Introduction

I, Wayne Beaton, was born on February 11, 1935, into a Seventh-day Adventist family. We lived in a rural town in Ontario, Canada. In 1936 we moved to a 10-acre farm that included a house and barn. There was plenty of space for large gardens, and soon we grew food for the family and had a source of cash as well.

When I was four years old World War II erupted in Europe, and mother opened a summer retreat for children from Toronto whose parents had been separated because of the war and service in the armed forces. Many children came to live with us over the next several years.

By the end of the World War II, our family moved to a farm with a large orchard. The family prospered and at age seventeen, in 1951, I decided to return to school after a five-year absence. I worked hard and was able to finance my own education at the boarding schools I attended in Canada and then in the United States.

In 1964 I graduated from Loma Linda University with the degree of Doctor of Medicine. Upon completing my training, I immediately returned to Ontario, Canada. I practiced as a family physician until 2011, when I felt it was time to change my focus from medicine to another field.

In retirement I felt inspired to publish the many thoughts that dominated my mind. I have learned many things from people over the years, and it was my desire to share some of these insights through the printed word. Some topics I researched and learned more about while others are based on my personal experience. My studies in the Holy Bible have also been a great source of inspiration and insight for this book.

As of 2012 I am proud to say that I am a cancer survivor. I have a beautiful wife, Anne, seven children, and eight grandchildren. I am anticipating a more leisurely life now, and I plan to enjoy traveling, visiting friends, and just spending quality time at home with my loving wife.

I hope you are inspired and blessed by the short stories and thoughts in this book. God bless!

A Merry Heart

"A merry heart doeth good like a medicine" (Prov. 17:22). In this text "merry" means blithe, gleeful, joyful, or glad. The heart is the seat of emotions, and "medicine" refers to a "cure."

A merry heart does great things for the whole being. One heals faster physically, and others see your happiness, which influences them in a positive way. The prevention and cure for many illnesses is a healthy mind. One's mind leads one in many directions, which can be unhealthy unless it is purposefully connected to God, the source of all wisdom.

We have five senses which, when operating correctly, have the ability to warn us when danger lurks. They also tell us when all is safe again. Healing is the result of overcoming danger, or damage, to the soul. All healing comes from God who, if we ask it of Him, has control over all our faculties. When we choose to accept His healing, we recover and are strengthen for the future. Healing is a gift from God. He is eager to heal and desires that we choose Him and ask for that healing.

Proverbs 16:20 says, "He that handleth a matter wisely shall find good: and whoso trusteth in the LORD, happy is he." By studying God's Word and by following Jesus' example, we show that we are His chosen people. His Spirit is with us to guide us in making better choices, to have happiness and joy as we never thought possible.

Being Human or Human Being

Human and *being* are two separate words and must be examined separately. One must determine the meanings of these words in order to grasp the scope of what is involved. To be human is to live in response to all that happens to us or around us.

Humanity has many positive aspects in that it gives one the opportunity to develop relationships. Humanity gives us the choices we make about the way we live whether by our own experiences or by learning from others. Making choices through study and observation allows us to develop a belief system that will hopefully grow and make us better citizens who will be compassionate toward others.

There have been wise people in every age, and I am convinced that we have survived this long because of their good choices. We have developed faith by learning about those who have chosen well in the past. The hope we have for the future is dependent on God's promises and on our choices today. The present is the only time we have to en-sure our future well-being.

Our time on this earth allows us to ask ques-tions and receive answers, have company along the way, and help someone in need. It is a fact that all humanity is not good, and it becomes extremely important to make choices that will assure us of an upward climb.

Being, on the other hand, refers to life as created by God. Being is your life, the thing that makes you, you. It is your body, mind, and soul, which is quite different from all the humanity around you.

An example of the separateness of human and being is in the life of someone who has a handicap of some sort and who lives a full and happy life as though he or she has no handicap. If one allows humanity to rule one's life, there may develop all sorts of aberrations or illnesses that may destroy the potentially happy life. It is important we realize that *being* is the part of us that is our gift from God and makes us unique in the universe. We are *beings* in the universe, and our little world in the universe is filled with *humanity*, with its things, conditions, good and evil, smiles and sadness.

We do not know how long we will live, but whether brief or long, that life is ours. We have come to believe that through modern medicine we keep our bodies alive, but that is untrue. God sustains our bodies, and thus keeps us alive. The brain is the computer that runs all the body functions. When something happens to disable or confuse the "computer," we become ill and may lose the life we love so preciously.

But we do play an important role in giving our bodies the best chance possible to live. It is imperative that we put only good things into our bodies. The good things include good thoughts, good foods, good sights, good sounds, good feelings, and a good outlook on life. We cannot ignore *humanity,* but we can choose our response to it. There is an innate part of us that needs an association with other humans. We seek to find others who are compatible with similar aims and ideals, and when we are successful, we make an effort to develop a relationship with that person.

There are some individuals who, through no fault of their own, have been damaged and cannot or do not develop relationships with other humans. Sadly, these people are always struggling to find happiness. This affects all areas of their life, including work, family, and volunteer work. Everything and everyone in the world seems to be a source of disappointment and sadness. Such a person has not been able to, or has not had the opportunity to experience, being able to separate *being* from *humanity.*

Being has a spiritual element, and those who recognize their being as separate from all the external pressures and stresses of life have a more positive outlook on life. They are also happier and reach goals that others see as impossible.

Human beings are not perfect, but we have one example of perfection in humanity. Jesus Christ was born as a human being and was the only perfect example we have in earth's history. Imperfect as we are, we can reach a higher level of existence when we realize the power of God in our *being* and the strength we have at our disposal. We must be willing to develop a faith relationship with the Source of that power in order to benefit from it.

We develop faith for the present and hope for the future, and we learn to love where we are. Then we can "bloom where we are planted" as the saying goes. Time has three phases, past, present, and future. The present is the only time in life when we can make decisions. With faith in God, we can have hope for the future and we can presently have a life filled with true happiness.

Born Again

I remember a Sabbath School teacher asking me, "Do you remember being born?"

I thought it was a strange question. Of course, no one can remember his or her birth.

But I pondered the question for several days and concluded that God, in His wisdom, chose "birth" as the term for entering life and "born again" as the symbol for entering a new life. In order to enter the family of God, Jesus said, "Ye must be born again" (John 3:7). And specifically, Jesus said that "except a man be born of water and of the Spirit, he cannot enter into the kingdom of God" (verse 5).

During the months prior to being born, each of us developed and grew in a watery environment. When we took our first breath at birth, we entered an entirely new experience. As we grew we realized how impure things really were. There were many times of sorrow and pain. We learned that there is a better life ahead, and many of us decided to do what was needed in order to get to that better place. We learned about Jesus and His sacrifice, and we decided to follow Him so we could be with Him in His kingdom. The change we experienced as we left the old life behind and started the new is called being born again.

Baptism, the symbol of new birth, is so very

much like our first birth. As one comes up out of the water and takes that first breath, the new life in Christ begins. The new life has new potential, much greater than the old. In symbol and in reality, we are able to begin eternal life here in this life, because Jesus made it all possible. Through prayer and study, we can have the assurance of everlasting life with Jesus, our Creator and Savior.

Life With Meaning

Life is about finding meaning for our existence. Words convey meaning and help us to grasp new concepts, whereas sight allows us to appreciate the beauties of creation and the vastness of it. You cannot help but stand in awe when you think of the planning, power, and wisdom it took in order to put this world in place and give us life so we can enjoy it.

Our hearing and speech allows us to communicate verbally and audibly. Our ability to touch and feel gives us such responses as gentleness and harshness. Almost 90 percent of our communication is nonverbal and is accomplished by body language. Love and hate can be sensed better nonverbally than when verbally expressed. It can be sensed in a person who is deceitful when expressing one emotion and secretly feeling another.

Trust is based on experience, as is faith. Genuine compassion for others is possible only when one possesses love. Each person is given unconditional love by his or her parent, and as one matures, he or she realizes that love comes to the parent from the God of love, our Creator.

If love is withheld or severed in childhood, it is very difficult, but not impossible, to regain. Distrust clouds all the senses and makes one's existence painful and ugly, and it results in miserable insecurity.

It has been said that some of us have to be flat on our backs before we look up, and another said that in order to get us on our knees, we sometimes must carry heavy burdens. When we realize that the only way to live and appreciate life to the fullest is to re-establish contact with our Creator, we have reached solid ground again.

Everyone desires peace, but only some of us know how to get it. "The peace of God, which passeth all understanding" is only possible in trusting in the Source of peace (Phil. 4:7). With the wisdom and understanding of our Creator at our side at all times and in every situation, one can experience peace.

When God said, "My grace is sufficient for thee" (2 Cor. 12:9), He was saying that He is stronger than whatever demon is attacking us, and He will cast out the demon when we ask for help in His name. Asking in Jesus' name assumes that one believes in Him. Believing is a combination of trusting and obeying God. This produces faith, and as faith grows we can and will be free of demons. We will have peace. We will be complete. And we will feel loved and free.

Made in the Image of God

In Genesis 1 God said, "Let us make man in our image" (verse 26). The word "our" refers to the Trinity—the Father, the Son, and the Holy Spirit. In humanity there are also three parts to the whole. There is the body, mind, and soul. People were created a little lower than the angels and with special qualities. One gift is the freedom of choice, which humanity must use in order to freely choose to be with God or the father of lies. Life comes from the love and power of God, and humanity was warned that without God they would surely die. Choice means trusting and obeying the one chosen.

In the Garden of Eden after our first parents failed their first and only test of obedience, God pronounced judgment on the serpent, Satan, and introduced grace to Adam and Eve. God initiated the sacrificial system that pointed forward to the time when Jesus would, by His sacrifice, die for the sins of the world. When we accept Jesus' sacrifice for us, we have the assurance of eternal life.

The Trinity is a difficult idea to grasp for most people. But consider this, Jesus said that He and the Father are one. It was the spirit of God that was sent as the Comforter so that God could always be with us after Jesus returned to heaven. The spirit and the breath are one, meaning that God is actually in us keeping us alive. We have the ability to go to God and access His power and love. We must choose, trust, and obey God if we are to exercise the gifts that are available to us at all times.

Creativity

Genesis 1:1 says, "In the beginning God created." Shortly thereafter in verse 26, we find the account of God creating "man in our image" or likeness. In God's creative power, He formed the universe and all that is in it, including human beings. We are blessed with many gifts and the ability to develop talents that are often displayed in the form of creativity.

Creativity can be seen in many areas from beautiful buildings, paintings, and music to parents who lovingly inspire their children to be productive adults. Creativity is also found in those who plant beautiful gardens and decorate beautiful homes. The only prerequisite necessary in order to be creative is to have beauty within and have a connection with the source of beauty, our Creator God. With this foundation we will be given visions of our potential. When one realizes the gift and accepts the challenge of creativity, a new chapter is created in that life.

Humanity can only create from the materials that God has provided. Only by inspiration and enlightenment from the Creator can new and useful items be created. In the past two centuries there have been monumental advances in transportation, energy, communication, and nutrition thanks to the wisdom and creativity imparted to people from God.

Unfortunately, since sin is present in our world, every positive advancement has been followed by a distortion of the usefulness of the item, thus sin intends to destroy the blessings we gain. Many people today live in confusion and are not able to see that God is the source of all wisdom. Some blindly live in a world without God and use His creations to their own glory, thus their work is evil.

As we recognize and honor God for all His gifts to us, we are filled with gratitude. When one sees a child drawing a picture or singing a little tune, it is a revelation of His continuing blessings to new generations.

Home Sick

When I was younger and away from home, there were many times when I was very homesick. I loved my family, and in my dreams I stayed connected with them. My brother Robert was quite young, and Brenda, my sister, was only one year old when I went west. Clare had always been a faithful brother and was always kind and helpful. My mother was a warm and loving person and much of her instruction guided me through life. Although I interpreted Dad as not being as open and close, he had high morals and was a good provider and protector of Mom. Rose and Ivadelle, my other sisters, appeared in my dreams as laughing, happy, and beautiful girls. Ron was with me at Canadian Union College (CUC), and he always pushed me to work and study harder.

Other nights I dreamed of being in class and failing—I was definitely afraid of failing. Maybe that was why I tried so hard to do well. After two years I left school to work in a hospital in Calgary.

After a time I returned to Ontario, and I finished my first two years of college at Kingsway College in Oshawa. I was reunited with my parents and siblings and all appeared to be as it should be. Ron and Clare had been running a sod business, and I worked with them that summer. Rose had gotten married, and Ivadelle was working in Barrie. Robert was a funny little boy and had several things to show me, including standing on his head. Brenda was a beautiful girl with a winning smile.

After two years in Oshawa, I went west again and enrolled at Walla Walla College in order to prepare for my future training in medicine. My time was filled with studies, and it overshadowed the loneliness of being so far away from my parents and siblings. Two years at Walla Walla and a summer school at their biological station at Rosario Beach in Washington state, and I was prepared to move south to California to begin medical school at Loma Linda University. Thus I embarked on four years of hard work, but along the way there were many blessings and a final reward of a degree in medicine and the title of doctor.

After spending six years away from home, I was ready to go back to Ontario. By now I was a different person, and I felt ready for a great life. Many moons have passed, and I have learned many lessons. I am finally not homesick anymore. Now I have a beautiful family, a loving wife, the blessings of success in my career, and most importantly, the Comforter is with me. Retirement is retaking life, and I intend to enjoy every day of it.

In the autumn of 2009, I had a dream. Our whole family was together in heaven. The house looked small as we arrived, but upon entering the dwelling, the rooms seemed to get larger as more rooms were required. Dad looked great, and Mom was busy in the dining room. As each family member arrived, the house grew to accommodate the extra people. I gave Dad a big bear hug and twirled him around before putting him down. He looked so happy that everyone was coming. No one was lonely anymore. I'm ready for that.

Eternal Life Is a Time Limited Offer

Our future is based on past knowledge, experiences, and decisions. Life's three entities are written as faith, hope, and charity (love). These three form a triangle, and at the top is love. If any of these three is defective, the whole system is in jeopardy.

Faith from our past experiences is necessary in order to believe and trust. Hope grows from what we have learned. Charity (love) impacts us in positive ways. When these three are in harmony, they nurture each other, and the balance brings joy and peace.

Why then is love the most important? Jesus stated that the two great commandments are love to God and love to humanity (our neighbors). It appears that love is the key to faith and hope. Love cannot be received or given unless there is a connection to the Source of love—God. Love is the most important of the three because it has an inherent connection to the present. The reception or giving of love is not possible in the past or the future. It must be an act in the present, right now.

The present is also the only time when we can make decisions and plan for our eternal life. Jesus said that we must "choose you this day whom ye will serve" (Joshua 24:15). Yesterday is too late, and tomorrow is out of our reach.

Faith and Healing

We know not the day or the hour when the Master chooses to test our faith. God states that He chastens those whom He loves and heals them. The chastening may come suddenly and without any warning. God asks us to be ready and prepared for such an occurrence at all times.

A day may begin as routine, but it may change in a moment of time. The change may appear to be life threatening. The first call for help is preferably to our Creator, followed by a call to someone close by or emergency personnel. That "call" or prayer to our Creator places us in His care, and we have the assurance of the best outcome to the problem.

When we find ourselves in a hospital setting, it is a blessing to ask God to guide the hands and minds of those who are caring for us. The knowledge that God is in charge is comforting to the soul. Experiencing help and healing reveals God's re-creative power in us, and we feel His closeness and loving care.

The story that follows documents the medical miracles I experienced over seven years. In 2003 I developed a discomfort in my abdomen, and after a few days of pain, I was convinced I should check it out. I had an ultrasound examination of my gallbladder, which revealed a solitary stone measuring six centimeters. That is almost the size of a tennis ball. That was on a Friday, and after an uneventful weekend, I contacted a surgeon on Monday and explained my problem. The surgeon was emphatic about removing the gallbladder that same day. I canceled my office appointments, went to surgery, and by 4:00 p.m. I was waking up in the recovery room. Surgery had been attempted by endoscope, but the gallbladder was disintegrating, so they cut me open. The pathology report showed gangrene, and the surgeon estimated I would not have lived more than two weeks if I had delayed the surgery. I recovered rapidly and returned to work after a two-week period of rest.

For the next seven years my health was very good, but on May 23, 2010, there was a sudden change. Anne and I had taken our friends Keith and Glenda Madgwick out for lunch in Newcastle, Ontario. We had just finished eating when I was overtaken by severe muscle spasms in my whole body. I could hardly speak and was only able to walk with extreme effort. I moved slowly outdoors into the sunlight and felt some improvement. Anne drove me home where I rested, and within three hours I had completely recovered.

Anne and I decided to have this incident investigated, and we enlisted the aid of a neurologist. After an examination including MRIs of my head and neck, plus an EEG, no dysfunction was found, so it was his conclusion that the cause of my problem was in the food. The only food that was different from our usual diet was the fresh spinach. On checking with the Department of Agriculture, I found that as high as sixty-four chemicals may be found on spinach, including insecticides, pesticides, and fertilizers. I felt that one of those chemicals caused my problem that day, so now I do not eat fresh spinach. I believe that God was leading me away from a previously unrecognized danger.

Later in 2010, at the end of October, I developed a sudden, severe pain in my abdomen. It was so alarming that I had Anne take me to the emergency room at Bowmanville Hospital. I felt worse with each passing minute, and to my relief, the surgeon whom I had assisted for over a year arrived at my side. Dr. Hamour ordered a CT scan of my abdomen and found a bowel obstruction with no evidence of a tumor. He wisely decompressed the obstruction, and after four days he was ready to operate. During surgery he cut the adhesion that was present from my 2003 surgery. Recovery was very rapid, but the report on the CT scan came back with the news that there was a small irregularity in the lining of my urinary bladder.

The doctor sent me to a urologist, and in one week I was in surgery and had the lesion removed. It was found to be small, superficial, and malignant, but it was completely removed according to the examiner. During the surgery the urologist noted that my bladder was severely distended by my enlarged prostate gland. Two weeks later I had my prostate reduced in size. The pathology report showed that in the material removed there was a tiny focus of cancer. It, too, had been removed. In early December I was again in surgery, but this was to check the condition of the bowel following the previous surgery on the obstruction. All was well. I still have to have routine checks on my bladder over the next two years before I am considered cured.

The sequence of these events is not without significance. Without the gallbladder surgery, the adhesion would not have been present, the bowel obstruction would not have occurred, the CT scan of the abdomen would not have been ordered, the bladder cancer and the prostate cancers would not have been found, and I would have been in a life-threatening situation in the near future.

All these checkups and surgeries tell me that there is definitely a God, and He uses all of our experiences to lead us closer to Him. His love is manifested in many ways, and our faith grows every time we have such an experience. Today in 2012 I am reportedly cancer free and enjoying my blessings each day.

Our Plumb Line

Amos 7:7, 8 provides us with a visual picture of the Lord standing on a wall holding a plumb line in His hand. Jesus was prepared to guide Israel in its growth to become a great nation of God. He used the analogy of a wall as part of a building to represent a nation. A perfect wall must extend straight up from the foundation. Any variation from true vertical can jeopardize the structure and leave it weak, which may result in inevitable collapse.

Spiritually, the building we are constructing is our life. We are part of God's temple and His kingdom. Only with God's help, by Jesus holding the plumb line and guiding our way, can we be sure that our growth will result in a perfect edifice in His kingdom. Such a life will not buckle under pressure or fall under stress. As we grow day by day, our view of Jesus and His guiding hands assures our success. Jesus' recipe for success in our building is found in the New Testament. We must communicate with Him at all times as He commands us to "pray without ceasing" (1 Thess. 5:17). He has given us the Bible to study as we go through life. The Bible says, "Study to shew thyself approved" (2 Tim. 2:15). And when we have mastered that, Jesus wishes for us to tell someone else about our success.

Jesus holds the plumb line for each of us, and He invites us to be constantly studying His plan for our lives in order that we do not falter and become distracted. His plan is true and solid as a rock. By these steps we shall build a life that will endure the storms and stresses of life and will remain perfect and beautiful forever as a specimen of God's lovingkindness.

Life, Alive, and Living

Life happens when the heart begins to beat, which occurs about three weeks into pregnancy. The heart sends blood to the brain to give it oxygen and nourishment so it can begin its work of controlling the body, which is beginning to grow. Life is a miracle. No one has ever seen the beginning of life, but there are some who are concerned about when life really begins. Is it when the heart starts to beat or is it when the baby takes its first breath?

There is no life without breath; however, in the case of a growing baby, the mother supplies oxygen and nourishment to the fetus for nine months without the baby taking a single breath.

One moves onto the next phase from life to alive, once the baby takes its first breath and has no more need for the mother to supply its needs via her blood. Now the baby is on its own and is alive. Being alive results in many issues and developmental steps. Firstly, the infant can express very few needs and can only respond to different comfort levels. Growth is evident in all areas and facets of life, and being alive is the response to various stimuli whether comforting or painful.

A baby matures to a child when it can speak and

communicate at a better level. Even now the child is immature and unable to make wise choices, not being able to realize the consequences of its decisions. The next level of development is that of youth. The young person is full of energy and welcomes all new experiences. The young person tries to make decisions of greater importance, but lacks wisdom to succeed, so he or she needs guidance in all areas.

Adulthood is the time when a person has the wisdom to make good decisions and the ability to carry them out. They can judge the consequences of their decisions and can avoid many pitfalls if their parents have given them the tools to make good decisions. This is living.

Positive and negative choices are made depending on what education the person has received up to that time. If the person has been fortunate enough to have Christian parents, decisions will be based on scriptural guidance and prayer. Young adults realize that they have many avenues open to them, and they may explore several before settling on a final course. It has been said that a young person feels they can do many things. By forty years of age, the person narrows the field to one area of expertise. Then by sixty the person feels fortunate that they were able to do one thing well. In the retirement years one looks back and sees all the things one could have done, the one thing accomplished, and they thank God for the things they avoided.

No one can give perfect guidance to their off-spring, but Christian parents provide children with a far greater potential for true successes than the home without the help of God.

Food for Thought

God created the plants, herbs, trees, clean and unclean animals, fish, and birds. Our all-knowing God created a wide variety of natural food sources for Adam and Eve.

Very soon after our original parents sinned, God explained the seriousness of their choice to them and demonstrated what the consequences of their actions had brought about. Killing the lamb and using the skins to clothe them must have been overwhelming.

Sin spread in the first family as it grew and populated the world. The plan of salvation was passed down from generation to generation by word of mouth. When the people turned away from God and determined to work out their own salvation, God decided to save the remnant of believers and start over again. As a result of the vast changes caused by the flood to the environment and food supply, God allowed for some changes to humanity's diet, which permitted them eating the flesh of clean animals, birds, and fishes. For generations the guidelines for acceptable diet were passed down from father to son until God asked Moses to write them down for posterity.

But we recognize God's concern for our health when He told Moses that the fat of the animal was

His and it was to be burned on the altar. God was protecting His children from the affects of high cholesterol. It was customary for the priests and the family of the one sacrificing the animal, to eat of the flesh of the animal.

We have no record of what Jesus ate; however, He prepared breakfast for His disciples after His resurrection, and part of that meal was fish that Jesus had prepared on a fire.

Ellen G. White wrote that in the future people would eat less meat because of disease. Was this because the meat is diseased or that the meat causes disease or that diseased people should eat less flesh foods? Less is better for any of these reasons.

A healthy diet requires a balance of carbohydrates, proteins, and fats. If one can arrange their diet to include all the essential amino acids, omega 3 oils, and compound carbohydrates without the use of flesh foods, they may live longer and healthier as recently reported in a study of a large group of Seventh-day Adventists in California.

The variety of healthy fruits and vegetables is so abundant that many of us have never tasted most of them. Variety is the key to a good diet because it assures us that we get foods from a multitude of places on earth, eliminating the chance that some foods are grown on deficient soils. Our brain requires carbohydrates for its activity, and our bodies use the nutrients from all three sources in order to function efficiently. Returning to nature is good advice and helps us use less refined foods. When we are careful about what enters our bodies, we are blessed with health, and life is beautiful.

Healing Hands

The expressions of all things good were in Jesus' hands while on this earth. His hands were powerful because they expressed God's love in so many ways. His hands touched children, women, and men. He blessed the poor and the spiritually needy. One can see Jesus' hands reaching up in praise and prayer. His hands blessed the food for thousands and for a few. He healed with His touch and raised several from the sleep of death. Jesus made a special call to all those with whom He associated and taught. As was His custom, He opened the Scriptures and read in the temple on Sabbath. Jesus had access to the power of His Father, the same source we all have when we seek Him.

I was excited to hear and understand that Jesus' presence among us was not to show what God can do, but what humanity can do through faith and obedience to God. Jesus became human, and through His sacrifice and resurrection, He made available to all humanity the power of heaven. Jesus' sacrifice makes it possible, by our choice and faith, for us to stand on heaven's tableland in the presence of God with a clean slate. Only Jesus' perfect love, when applied to us through faith, can clear our record and give us freedom from sin.

Since we are made in the image of God, we have the privilege, through faith and obedience, to do what Jesus did. We can teach, feed, heal, uplift, visit the sick, inform, encourage, and point souls to God. By doing these things, we can create a new environment for those in need, spiritually and physically. When we are ready, prepared, and dedicated, to His service, He will produce the opportunities for us to do great things in His name. We are a blessing to God when we trust and obey Him. Our faith shall make us free, and our hopes will be fulfilled as we walk hand in hand with our Savior, who is "the way, the truth, and the life" (John 14:6).

Health and Happiness

"Beloved, I wish above all things that thou mayest prosper and be in health, even as thy soul prospereth" (3 John 2). In this statement John is saying that as the soul prospers so does your health and wealth. In this context, health includes (1) an uncorrupt mind, (2) a sound body, and (3) a soul true in doctrine. Health encompasses all aspects of our being—physical, emotional, and spiritual. None of these stand alone. A deficiency in one unbalances the others, but the strength of each strengthens the others.

In Bible times it was thought by many that ill health or catastrophe was the result of that person's sin. That person might be shunned or worse because of this misunderstanding, especially if the condition was leprosy. Like Job, it is necessary to be connected by faith to the Source of healing and life in order to have the strength to overcome illness or disease.

In the search for happiness, some people attempt to gain it through such things as possessions, travel, popularity, and even crime. If happiness is not readily found, one might become greedier, angrier, or give up and become a recluse. Real joy and lasting happiness comes only when one is connected to the Source of all good gifts—the God of heaven. It is the spiritual part of our being that can strengthen the emotional and physical aspects of our being and bring peace to our souls, but we have to be connected to the Source of true love and mercy.

Not all of us have healthy physical bodies; however, a connection to the Fountain of living water will keep us so emotionally and spiritually healthy that we can live and influence others positively so that they, too, may develop a faith in God. The wealth that we yearn for is not really found in material wealth but in faith, relationships, and peace of mind.

There are some among us who have never felt love, whether by poor environment or circumstances, and we wonder what we can do to help them. Compassionate love has healing power and is a cure-all for many of our ills. It has been said that love and healing are always possible even when a cure is not. When the soul is healed, the wounds, injuries, and heartaches are covered and taken away. Only God can do this for us because He fought and won the battle over the one who is the cause of all our grief. Through faith in our Creator, we know that the gift of everlasting love and perfect health awaits us in the near future.

Hearing and Listening

"He that hath ears to hear, let him hear" (Matt. 11:15). Ears are not essential for life; however, they are essential for living. Hearing is necessary for one to function socially, to discern messages, and to solve problems. We have ears in order to hear. These appendages are capable of intercepting sounds of every type and intensity and transmitting them to the brain. But the sounds are of no value until they are analyzed by the brain. Our response to these stimuli depends on what information we have previously stored in our memory cells. Our ears were created by God for the purpose of communicating with each other.

It is good to realize that we can hear without listening, and we can listen without hearing. A doorbell or telephone ringing are examples of hearing without listening. When one answers a telephone and listens for a response but it never comes, they are listening but not hearing.

When we pray and ask God for an answer, we must listen to the silence, for in that silence we will hear the voice of God in our brain as though it were spoken aloud. God answers prayer, and we must be in the attitude of prayer in order to discern the answers to our requests. This was explained to us in the record of Elijah and the way he received a message from God.

As the noises in our lives and surroundings increase, our lives become more complicated and our hearing is bombarded so that we do not have the same ability to hear what we should. It takes deliberate effort to return to listening to the silence in order to hear the "still small voice" of God (1 Kings 19:12).

True Colors

It is the month of October, and the leaves on the beautiful maple tree in our yard are gently swaying in the warm autumn breeze. The leaves are almost glowing in a variety of brilliant colors. There are shades of red, orange, yellow, and green in the foliage. This change in color each autumn produces a beautiful tapestry of color in the countryside. Why do the leaves change color? The green of the summer foliage represents the health, growth, and vitality of the tree. Green is what we see in spring and summer.

In autumn when the hours of sunlight shorten, the trees prepare for the winter ahead. There are specific steps the trees must take in preparation for rest. The growth cycle is drawn to a close when tiny valve-like structures in the base of each leaf close, thus stopping the production of chlorophyll. The chemical chlorophyll produces the green color of the leaves. Once the chlorophyll production has shut down, there is a dramatic change in the color of the leaves. The color was there all the time, but it was hidden by the green hues. For a short time the tree forms buds as the leaves fall from the branches, and now the tree rests. When spring arrives and the days grow longer and warmer, the buds break and immediately turn green, thus hiding those beautiful colors from our view until the next autumn.

We, human beings, reveal to those around us, only that which we wish them to see. This is what is known as our persona, our mask. Our real color, our character, is rarely seen by many. Our true colors are always present, but only our Creator has the power to see them. Our character is as an autumn leaf to God. Our hues depend on our experiences, and the renewing of our faith makes the colors vivid. Our life and sustenance come from God. Our life season may vary depending on how much nourishment we glean freely from Christ.

May our roots feed deeply in the spiritual food available to us so our colors will shine brightly to those around us.

Nourishment for the Soul

One day a well-intentioned person who had just returned from giving a Bible study claimed to have given the recipient the whole Seventh-day Adventist message in that one sitting. The person was disappointed because the recipient did not accept the message.

This made me think about a physical parallel. If one were provided with a whole meal and asked to swallow it in one mouthful, it would be impossible and even dangerous. There are good reasons for taking small bites of food.

We are told that we should study with the intention of accepting what is good and rejecting that which is not. Food must be broken down into small fragments in order to be of value to us, and the useless portion is eliminated. We taste our food to find the good, and in the Bible we are told to test everything and accept only the good. Spiritual growth is gradual, and careful study is required. Fortunately, we have the written word of God to aid us in our journey.

Our Physical Covering

Our skin is our covering, and what a wonderful envelope to be in. The skin is our largest organ, and it has several functions. It responds to light and warns us when we are careless with sun exposure. It has an early warning system for dangers of many kinds. It can produce pain and pleasure, and it reflects to us the health of our bodies. This mantle, if we may call it that, can be damaged and can be repaired with loving care.

Our Creator has given us the opportunity to care for this body and its covering as a way to show our love for Him and His creation. One day when Jesus returns we shall be rewarded with a new mantle. This mantle will be perfect and will never grow old. This mantle will be our new body, which will be cloaked in God's righteousness.

Life's Coach

Life is not a game, however, there are a few items common to both. It is always wise to know the rules before attempting to play a game. It is very wise if one finds out the rules for life early on before running the risk of failing. To fail in a game may have some negative affects, but they are not lasting, whereas in life, not knowing the rules will surely cause much pain and this failure result in permanent loss. Fortunately, we have a coach, Jesus, who has promised to be with us for the whole journey.

One day I watched a couple working out on a flying trapeze. The master trapeze artist said there were three things that were absolutely necessary for their success: balance, timing, and not being afraid.

Balance is necessary for success in all fields of endeavor. There must be a balance between the physical, the intellectual, and the spiritual. Timing is important on the trapeze, for there can be no delay in the routine without failure and injury, even death. In life the time to choose life everlasting is now because a delay may cause one to move in a direction that may be disastrous. Not being afraid can only be accomplished by replacing fear with faith. When one has complete faith in the Master,

Jesus, one can take that leap of faith into the open arms of the Savior.

Fortunately, God has made it possible to have a second chance after a fall. God has arranged a safety net in the person of Jesus, so we can climb the ladder of life again and try once more to succeed.

Evidence of God's second chance is obvious in the record of the thief on the cross. To all present, the thief was lost and was about to die without hope. Because of his faith in Jesus, his life did not end without hope. Jesus saved him because of his faith. We have the same assurance as Jesus gave the thief. When we have faith in Jesus, we shall be saved.

The Touch

Of all the five senses touch can produce the most beautiful, loving, and caring feelings. On the other hand, it can be abusive, hurtful, and a source of fear. Jesus touched many souls during His ministry on earth. All were uplifted, healed, and made free from their afflictions, and everyone felt His love. Even the touching of the hem of His garment produced healing through faith. He went to those who could not physically come to Him and healed them because they had faith in His power of love.

Finally, Jesus' love was so great for us that he gave His life that all who call on His name may be healed of their afflictions. Even when enduring the pain He suffered physically and spiritually on the cross, Jesus responded in love to those around Him.

We were created in His image and have the opportunity to heal others by our words and touch. Hold a child who is in pain and feel the soothing and calming effect it has. Speak kindly to a person or hold their hand in love, and the person will be comforted.

A touch without love is considered inappropriate. It is felt as invasive, painful, and fearful. We must always be aware of the other person's state of being, careful not to invade someone's personal space, but available to offer help and love. Everyone who calls upon Jesus for help in time of need will feel His power, and hope will be renewed. We are assured that God loves us and cares deeply for our well-being. We have the assurance that He is just and will judge the one who causes harm to His children.

In your mind's eye imagine yourself safely in the arms of Jesus, feeling His love, a most beautiful feeling. Even now we have the assurance of Jesus' presence to heal us, uplift us, and invite us to a higher plane of existence than we can imagine.

Sunshine in My Soul

Memory is a strange part of living. From the cradle to the grave we accumulate and recollect experiences, which can be likened to the weather. We were nestled in a watery bed before we were born. At birth we opened our eyes to light so bright it could have been a bolt of lightening. The new sounds and voices sounded like thunder. We felt something touching us, and we cried out in distress in our new environment. Soon we were comforted by a warm being who held us and soothed us.

Endless new experiences have flooded our brain moment by moment, day by day, and year by year as we have grown. When all was happy and peaceful, it was as though the sun was shining, but when things changed to make us less happy, it was as if a cloud had covered the sun. There have been times when we experienced storms, calm, darkness, and sunshine, which are all a part of life. We have felt the nurturing and warmth of those who cared for us, and we have developed close contact with our parents, our siblings, and others of social compatibility. While growing, we learned we could love and care for others as was modeled for us by our family. We learned to appreciate the sunshine and to find ways to cope with the storms. There were times of fear and loneliness when relationships failed or a loved one passed away, and then there were times when we felt as if we could fly like a bird.

Our very best choices are made in the context of the sum of the experiences we can recollect from our past. When we understand where we came from, what we are doing here, and where we are going, we have arrived at a place where we may understand life better and what it holds for us.

It can be devastating when we realize one day that we have trusted someone who has turned out to be a traitor. At that time it feels as if our life is clouded over and plagued by rain, thunder, and lightning. The rain might blur our vision for a while, but the sun will shine again and happiness will return. It may return when we go to a loyal friend or reexamine our own thoughts and actions. We also receive help when we turn to the all-powerful One who put us here in the first place.

The miracle of birth, the pleasures and pain of living, and our place in the universe today are all part of our education. It seems only fair and sensible that when we have problems and questions we can obtain answers from the Author and Creator of our life.

Our life is not an accident; we are on this earth for a reason that we may not completely understand at this moment. However, as we study and appreciate what and who we are, we can see beyond the fog that attempts to confuse us. As we exercise our faith, develop a hope for the future, and live in the sunshine of God's love today, we find that our life is full and complete.

Through the Mind's Eye

Visual pictures are stored in memory cells in the cortex of the brain directly behind the eyes and close to the back of the head. We all can recall previous experiences and see the images in our mind. Dreams are made up of these stored visual pictures. Thus dreams can be beautiful or even sad, depending on past experiences in life, and there are some dreams that are impossible to understand. Some dreams have been called visions because they contain messages about the present and future.

What an inspiration it would be if we could see all the blessings we are receiving and have received from our Creator. God has made it possible for us to have these earthly dreams. Through the exercise of faith in God, we gain glimpses of a better place. God's sustaining grace is no less than the continuous, innumerable blessings poured upon us each day.

God does not limit His blessings to only those who presently choose Him and believe in the sacrifice He made for our redemption. He blesses all humanity, all the time. We would all cease to exist if God did not graciously sustain us. Sin is sin, and we all have sinned, so we are all under the condemnation of sin. We exist only by His sustaining grace and His compassion for us.

We wonder sometimes why God allows evil persons to go on living and causing pain to other people. God said, "Judge not, that ye be not judged" (Matt. 7:1). We must not become judges to consider one sin greater than another, for there is only one Judge. God said, "Revenge is mine." If our eyes were opened so we could really see sin in its reality, we would be sore afraid of our own condition. God allows sin to continue until the judgment day, otherwise He would have to eliminate the entire human race now.

Time is an element that gives every human being ample opportunity to choose where he or she will spend eternity. Time goes on in mercy because God loves us, even in our present condition. Time also makes it possible for those who love and are committed to serving God, to follow Jesus' example in spreading the good news of salvation to those who do not yet believe.

If we choose to follow Jesus, we are promised a future of wonderful experiences beyond anything we can imagine. Any other choice will result in death. It is important to understand both pictures and choose the way to life. In Psalm 23:1 it says, "the Lord is my shepherd; I shall not want." To not "need" would be good, but to not "want" means that we have everything we can imagine. We will not want in heaven. Our minds, bodies, and souls will be perfect. Our eyes will have perfect vision to see what we have never seen before. We will see Jesus in all His glory and majesty. What a blessing to have perfect vision in a perfect place with perfect friends.

Run and Win

Everyone desires a better existence. Everyone is running a race to improve one's self, to be the best one can be, to obtain a prize. In the Christian race, the goal is to reach heaven. Jesus has made it possible to reach that goal by His sacrifice. Jesus told His disciples that they should not be concerned with who would be the greatest, but to fully understand their status as sinners and how heaven is made possible for them. By believing and obeying God, as was Jesus' example, we are saved.

Not everyone realizes that there is a spiritual race to run or a goal to be achieved. For those who run the race, there is the privilege and even a duty to inform the uninformed of the blessings of running and winning. I felt reassured when I realized that no one will be lost by what one does not know or have. We will be judged on what we do with what we know and have. God does not give everyone five talents, or even two talents, but He expects us to wisely invest what He does give us.

There is a statement that says, "Many are called but few are chosen." I believe that those who are "called" include everyone for whom Jesus died. But the few chosen are those who choose Jesus and what He stands for. Not everyone will choose Jesus, but all will have the opportunity to do so.

We are invited to come to Jesus; then He will come to us. When we have the love of Jesus flowing from within us, we are a light unto the world because the light of heaven shines through us. The fruits of the Spirit are evident in those who are running the good race. We cannot lose when we serve Jesus.

Personality Plus

The word personality has as its root the word persona, which according to *New Oxford American Dictionary* means "the aspect of someone's character that is presented to or perceived by others." Another way to describe this is to compare it to a mask, which is an outward display. It has been said that "beauty is in the eye of the beholder." To some, looking good is inseparable from feeling good, and certainly looking good affects behavior.

One often misjudges a person by the visage one gets at first glance. Behind that persona is the real person, the character, and that is the real source of the person's beauty. The one who is genuinely compassionate, kind, and helpful will be considered beautiful, especially when the character and the persona are one.

It is a fact that billions of dollars are spent every year to keep the persona looking good while the body ages. Those who exercise the fruits of the Spirit have a beauty that surpasses all other attempts to look pleasing to their neighbors. When inner beauty is present, it is obvious, and it surpasses any adjustments one might make to his or her persona.

Everyone will have a perfect character in heaven, and one will not have to guess what really is inside. Won't that be a relief?

Pride and Humility

In the 1930s and 1940s many Christian parents understood that pride was a bad thing. They were careful not to praise their children too much in case it might go to their heads. As a result of this belief, many children never felt special. Self-esteem was a term not used in those days. So is pride such an evil thing? It was acceptable to do great things and recognize children for their abilities, but it was not spoken audibly. Many parents thought it might spoil the child or they might become a snob. They wished their child to be down-to-earth and not proud.

As usual, there is good pride and bad pride. The antonym of pride is humility. The question that presents itself is this: "Is it possible for pride and humility to exist together?" When a person recognizes his or her accomplishments and successes as gifts from God, a balance between pride and humility is established. One can, therefore, deduce that parental pride in their children and encouragement to seek high life goals is good. This is good only if the parents have taught their offspring that God is the source of all knowledge, power, and accomplishments. It is written that without God we can do nothing and that when we believe and ask Him for power and wisdom "all things are possible" (Mark 10:27).

God creates the balance between pride and humility. Turn to Him if you struggle with pride and humility.

Light in Darkness

Darkness has no power in itself. Darkness is the absence of light. It is in our lives and hides good things from our view. Darkness causes confusion, harm, and neglect. Light, in sharp contrast, is very powerful. The light of just one candle can disperse much darkness. Light can lead one to safety, avoiding pitfalls and enabling one to avoid hurt and injury.

Our journey through life requires light to show us the safe paths to follow. At some time in our lives, we might wish that we could see the whole path of our life. Wouldn't it make it easier to make good decisions? The question arises, just how much light do I really need in order to have an enlightened journey and arrive at my destination safely? We must learn how to use the light we have to the greatest advantage.

An example of our use of light may help clarify how light really works. Imagine that I find myself stranded at night on foot in total darkness. A fog settles in, and visibility is reduced to almost zero. I remember that I have a penlight in my backpack, so I retrieve it. Turning it on, I find that the path is illuminated in front of my feet for only about two feet, the distance of one step. I am about one mile from home, and I realize that I can navigate the path before me by stepping into that enlightened area just in front of my feet, one step at a time.

So it is in our life and salvation. All we really need to see, by faith, is one step at a time. As we take those individual steps in faith, our hope grows, and we are assured of reaching our heavenly home to be eternally safe in the wonderful light of our Savior's love.

Love and Hate

Everyone feels uplifted when love is experienced, and when we have love in us, we tend to share it. Jesus came to be with us in order to give us examples of what love can accomplish. Jesus reflected what God is—love.

At no time did Jesus express hatred toward humanity. God loves all His created beings, so much so that He gave His Son to fulfill the law of God in our place. Through Adam we have all been found guilty of breaking God's law, for which the penalty is death. Jesus' sacrifice paid that penalty for us so we can freely choose a new life with Him. Jesus' resurrection showed us that through Him we can have a new and perfect life when we believe and obey Him.

Jesus came to save sinners because He loves His creation. Jesus made it quite clear that He hates sin but loves the sinner. Everyone who chooses to follow Jesus becomes one of His chosen. He asks us to "choose you this day whom ye will serve" (Joshua 24:15).

Hatred then is not of a person but of the sin in that person. Hate is conditional. When the action or condition that caused the person to sin is acknowledged, confessed before God, and forgiven, it is cleared from the record as though it had never occurred. Human beings tend to remember sins forever, but God says that when He forgives the sin it is forgotten.

The worst response one can have to a sinner is that of indifference. If we just give up on sinners and leave them out in the dark, hungry and naked forever, we are not following Jesus' example. We must respond to our neighbors in the same manner as Jesus did, with love and compassion, pointing the person to healing, freedom from sin, and a better way of life.

Jesus gave us the greatest example of love, and He invites us to follow in His footsteps, realizing our sinful condition, accepting His salvation, and having the hope of eternal life.

Mountains

Why do we stand in awe when we see a mountain? Is it the height of it, the massive size of it, or its decor? Yes, it is much more than a huge pile of rocks and dirt with snow on top. To some, it is an obstacle to progress, a block to their view and passage.

To Christians, mountains hold many awe-inspiring visions. There it is, a great rock, solid and immoveable, regal in its own appearance, and clothed in a garb of many hues. From its summit flows water, a nutrient essential for life. It flows down in beautiful cascades and waterfalls to nourish all life at its base.

We do not worship the mountain, but its Creator, the source of all life and beauty. We observe God's great love and power in all that He has created and provides for us. Mountains are there to be climbed, so one can see more of God's creative power from its height. Both the Creator and the created mountain represent stability, power, beauty, and sustainability. Many of God's creatures live and thrive there.

Our life is like a journey up a mountain. The path before us is a joy if we keep the end in sight. The path is always upward, and our steps are part of our learning process. We are not alone as we climb, for we have a true Guide, Jesus, to help us not become distracted along the way. Faith in our Guide and commitment to the journey will help us reach our goal, which is heaven. Heaven's tableland is that beautiful place on God's holy mountain.

The climb to the tableland has steep areas, rocky parts, and rushing water to cross. Only by holding the hand of our Guide and keeping our focus on the goal will we reach heaven. Finally, we shall be safe, secure, and sustained in the hands of our Savior. The only prerequisite to being in this exquisite place is our choice, our faith, and our commitment to Jesus.

Home

I once heard a story of a woman who came upon a little girl playing with her dolls in the hallway of her apartment building. The woman stopped and watched for a moment, then she asked, "Why are you playing here in the hallway?" The girl answered that there wasn't enough room inside to play. The woman said in a saddened way, "It's too bad you don't have a home."

The little girl spoke up in as grown-up voice as she could. "Oh, we have a home, we just don't have a house to put it in."

What did she consider to be a "home"? It's what she knew was on the other side of that door to her small apartment. It was love, security, warmth, companionship, freedom to express herself, a feeling of acceptance, respect, and value. Her home had created a "wholeness" in her, and she was well equipped to make positive statements in its defense.

There are many expressions in our language that employ the word "home" as the most meaningful word. The following is a partial list of those sayings.

- Home is where the heart is
- A house is not a home
- Home cooked meals

- Homeward bound
- Home free
- Home run
- Homemade
- It's good to be home

This special word invites one to look at its source, but let's look at a word that is oftentimes mistakenly used in place of "home." The word is "house." House can be a shelter for humans or beast. For animals it can be a barn. For people it can be a simple shelter such as a tent or cabin or it can be a fancy structure such as a mansion. A shelter is not a home. A home has qualities that a house can never have. The little girl in the hallway had a real home.

A home, in contrast to a house, is not just a dwelling place. Home is where relationships are created, sustained, and healed. Home is the result of loving and caring for a spouse and children. Home is a place of beginnings, a source for life, a continuum of loving, caring relationships from which complete and mature persons emerge to create new homes. From these homes evolve the family, the community, and neighborhood. A civilization consisting of loving homes would be a really blessed place to be.

Then the question is, "Why do we have so much disharmony and undoing of the home?" A long time ago an enemy entered the domain of the human race and sowed the seeds of discord and hatred, which led to many abuses. This evil scourge spread as a deadly virus throughout our world to the extent that families are split, communities have no trust, and countries fight for power and control

Home has healing qualities and now is the time to heal the wounds that the evil one has caused or complete destruction will happen to the "home" as we know it. Fortunately, there has been a plan in place for a long time for the healing of the nations. That healing begins at home with God's love as the basis for all solutions. When our Savior's final plan is fulfilled, the home will be the sacred institution it was in the beginning. The community will be established on love, and the whole universe will be in harmony once more.

It Is Finished

What was the "it" that Jesus was referring to as He breathed His last breaths while hanging on the cross? *It* refers to the plan of salvation, which was established before this world was created. Jesus was prepared to make the supreme sacrifice in order to save His creation. The all-knowing God knew what had to be done to save humanity as soon as they were created. *It* refers to living a perfect life, paying the penalty for our sin, dying, and being raised again so that we have the hope of everlasting life. Our first parents failed the only test of their faithfulness to God. They were given full freedom whether to obey or disobey God. Their disobedience led to the penalty of death.

Is refers to time itself. *Is* refers to the present, the now. The plan of salvation was fully in place at the cross. Jesus was resurrected because being sinless, as He was, the tomb had no hold on Him.

Finished refers to completed, concluded, discharged as a debt. In his writings Paul said, "I have fought a good fight, I have finished my course, I have kept the faith" (2 Tim. 4:7). Paul had won the battle with sin, he had run the race and won, and he had kept the faith of Jesus. The faith he referred to was the constant reliance upon Christ for salvation. Let us keep the faith, and we will hear the cheers when we have run the race and won, and we will have the promise of a place in eternity with Jesus.

A Shining Light

At some point and time in our life we may have wished to be recognized for something great. We may have attempted to do something special in order to get that medal, plaque, or public praise. Many seniors, in their later years, regret that they have not done enough and are concerned for their final reward.

How much must one *do* to be saved? The answer is quite simple. Jesus said that without Him we can accomplish nothing. Only by what He did for us are we saved. Our life is to reflect our belief, our faith, and our dedication to Jesus. Only then are our actions a blessing and our works saving.

Jesus said that whatever you do to the least of these you have done unto Me. When we live the fruits of the Spirit we are a light to those who are in darkness and in need. Jesus counts this as following Him and believing in Him. Living the fruits of the Spirit has the reward of a glorious and eternal future.

Appreciation and praise from our peers is favorable and makes us happy, but more important and lasting is the "well done" proclamation of our Savior. All present fame is but a mere fleeting shadow of what is in store for us when we are committed to Christ and are obedient to His commands.

Life Restored

Seeds hold the potential for renewing life. The parent plant produces a seed that holds all the information required to generate a new and identical plant. After a period of time, in a state that can be equated to death or sleep, when conditions become favorable, the seed comes to life and grows into a new plant.

In the human family there exists a system for regeneration. The seed holds all the information necessary to produce human offspring. In the new plant and the new baby, there are special requirements for successful growth and development. Light, water, and food plus the correct environment must be present for both plant and baby. In the human family, the parents have the responsibility of providing education and training in order for the offspring to be able to meet all the variables, dangers, obstacles, and tests that come its way.

Jesus was born into a human family, known as the first advent, with all the qualities of a human except He had no bent toward sin. Jesus was and is God. Jesus' life was perfect, and although He died on the cross, death could not hold Him, so he rested on the Sabbath day and rose again to continue His work for humanity. All through His life on earth, Jesus made choices just like we must, and He chose to follow His Father's plan for His life.

Each one of us has been given a gift of free choice that we too may follow Jesus' plan for our lives and at the end of the age be with Him in heaven. Jesus is our example. We are urged to stay connected to God by praying without ceasing. We are urged to study to learn every day about God's plan for our lives. And when we understand what awaits His children, we are not to be quiet about it, but we are to tell the story to everyone.

Sands of Time

Time is difficult to visualize unless one can imagine time as a strip of soft sand stretching out to resemble one's lifetime. The imprints in the sand represent all our activities as steps leading up to the present time. Each day we live we make another print in the sand. We have all made our mark in history and have left a variety of prints in the sands of time. Being able to review our past, we can see where we have made advances, but there are places where we have gotten off course, faltered, fallen. When we have fallen, we have been helped back on the straight path again by the hand that came to our aid when we cried out for help. There were times that only Jesus' guidance saved us from destruction.

When we study about God, His power, and His perfect wisdom, we develop a faith in Him that guides our path onward and upward. We are able, through that faith, to accomplish a measure of what Jesus accomplished while among us. I was excited when I realized that Jesus did not come and live with us in order to show us what God could do. He came as a human being to show us what we can do through faith and obedience to God. Jesus' footprints give us the safe and sure path to follow for as long as we live. We have the choice of following His example and pattern for our lives. He blessed, healed, comforted, and taught. His footprints lead to heaven, and by His sacrifice on our behalf, we can follow His footprints in faith.

Pearls

Mollusks have the unique quality to make pearls from a grain of sand, bacteria, or a tiny organism that gets inside its shell. The mollusk covers the foreign body with a material that reduces the irritation. In the end a round, blue-gray colored stone, the pearl, is formed.

At least two conditions must be met in order to produce the pearl. There must be materials available and the irritant must not be fatal. It is amazing to realize that there are preset programs in the mollusk, and the programs are reliable and eager to respond to the stress.

As I was recently studying about Bible prophets, I thought I could find some parallel lessons from nature that tied into the role of these prophets.

God chose certain, special people to be His prophets and apostles. Many of those whom God chose felt that they were unfit or not capable of carrying out the commission asked of them. On their own, they would have rejected the calling. Only when they realized that God had called them, did they realize that they could succeed, and they accepted the call. The irritants they suffered in their work of the gospel, whether rejection, opposition, jealousies, or ill health, all caused the worker to draw closer to God. They depended wholly on divine help in order to persevere. Many prophets and apostles suffered physically and would have otherwise lost their way if not for God sustaining them.

As with the mollusk making a pearl, the prophets and apostles had to accept the threats to their safety and depend wholly on God to produce the power and fortitude to continue their work. They had to focus on the fact that with God they could do anything.

Jesus said that whatever we ask in His name, He will hear us and it will be done. In His name we are connected with God. We make the connection through prayer and study of His Word. When the petitioner has connected with God, positive changes take place and wisdom and power can flow from God to the willing worker, and the results will be far beyond our expectations. A pastor once said that our duty is to exercise faith and God will provide mercy.

Faith without works has no value because once one attains and exercises faith, there is no work that one cannot do. God's power and wisdom are endowed in such a person. Work that once was used to keep one's self alive now reaches out to keep others alive.

The lowly mollusk has no choice, no faith, and no memory. Its success is based entirely on God's choices for it. Today, through a sustaining faith in God, we can accept the irritations that attempt to defeat us and grow in faith. We do not know what each day will bring, but through faith we have the reassurance that when we fight the good fight, leaning on our Creator, we will be as the mollusk and see precious human pearls prepared to meet their Creator.

Some of us have experienced miracles in our lives and have realized God's power directing our decisions and actions. The work we do may not seem important, but through patience and diligence, our faithful efforts will result in the preparation of many souls for the kingdom.

Perseverance

It was late January 2009 and freezing temperatures had settled onto Ontario. Anne and I had planned a trip to Florida and were on our way to the sunny south to enjoy the warmth and sandy beaches. Our trip was divided into three types of weather. We left Ontario and very cold temperatures, then we landed in a little warmer climate before reaching our final destination where it was very comfortable.

We were in the middle of our journey when we drove through an area where it had rained and the water had frozen to everything. The trees especially were covered with an inch of ice. As the ice had thickened, some of the trees were unable to withstand the load and had fallen to the ground. The majority of the trees stood there holding the load, but it was as if they were praying for help because all their branches were bent low and with treetops bowed they waited. The trees appeared to be exhausted from the strain placed on them, but they remained upright. It was obvious that they could not help themselves or solve their own predicament. Suddenly the sun shone from between the clouds, and there appeared a most spectacular sight. From each and every branch one could see millions of dazzling bright diamonds all the way to the horizon. It was as though, in our imagination, one could see into the trees and know that they were alive and waiting for deliverance.

This picture of faith and endurance made me think of the human family who at times are caused to carry great burdens not of their own choosing. These stressful burdens may be caused from loneliness, poverty, disease, disappointments, or fear, but there is still that spark of light in their spirit. That diamondlike spark in each of us is hope, and when we, like the trees, persevere, a miracle happens.

Again we observed the trees, and as they accepted the warmth of the sun, the burdens they bore began to melt away. Soon one could see the branches lighten and begin to bend upward again. They looked like arms, hands, and heads lifting upward, relieved of their loads of ice.

To us, the lesson we learned that day from that experience was that no matter what burdens we find ourselves to be bearing God places in each of us a measure of faith and hope that, if exercised, is enough to carry us through even the worst of difficulties. Faith, perseverance, and patience are key to assure us of deliverance. When we, through faith, accept the warmth of God's love, those burdens, like ice on the trees, will melt away. Then, like the trees, we can raise our heads and hands again and praise Him for His help in our time of need.

Once the load was lifted from the trees, they stood strong and healthy again and, figuratively, waved their branches in thanks to their Creator.

I am sure someone will ask, "What about all those trees that fell, unable to bear the terrible load of ice?" Only the One who created them can see the real cause of the failure to survive. As in the human family, the cause for winning or losing is not ours to judge.

Another lesson is obvious in this scene. The ice that caused so much stress melted and became an essential element for the sustenance of the tree. So too, with our burdens, they can end up being a blessing to us in our journey through life. One person said that there is no bad experience if one learns from it. The lessons may be hard, but with faith, patience, and endurance, the God of heaven helps us to become strong and firm in His love.

The trees that withstood the stress were also well rooted and well nourished, and they stood in the light, full of life. They did not cause the ice. The ice descended on them. So even if our lives are in harmony with the Creator, it does not mean that we are immune to burdensome stresses. It is our faith in God, our trust in our Savior, and our patience and endurance that will get us through to a place of peace and happiness again.

Finally, when Anne and I reached our destination, we looked out on green grass, palm trees, and peaceful waters, and we reflected on the many instances where God protected us on our journey and blesses us in our daily walk with Him.

Relationships

Most of us are taught that stability grows out of equilibrium and permanence. We learn that change may be dangerous and, therefore, should be avoided and that emotional upheaval should be minimized at all cost, for it threatens the continuity of a relationship. Would you believe the following statement? "The stable relationship is one that goes on from year to year—impregnable to any force that would try to change it".

The truth is that relationships are always changing, for we as individuals are constantly in a state of growth and flux as we move through our lives, and the capacity to deal with change in a positive fashion is a basic necessity in a strong, loving relationship.

Couples or family members who encounter difficulties are those who stubbornly resist change for fear that love may not be strong enough or sustaining enough to accommodate the unpredictable effects of change. Enduring relationships have the flexibility to greet change, not with fear but with acceptance and a positive attitude.

It is important to understand that those "bad times" do not mean that the relationship is deficient, but rather it signals some new change that those involved must make in a positive and flexible way. If we wish to have an alive and caring relationship, it is best to communicate that by acts and words of love. Asking what I have done lately for my partner or my family is much better than telling them what I would like to do.

Friendship

This discussion material has been drawn from many sources and much study of human relations. I do not claim these thoughts to be exclusively my own. The following discourse will analyze many facets of friendship and attempt to understand the process of being and making friends.

It is important to learn the root of the word friend. The root of the word is free. It comes to us through the Indo-European, the Anglo-Saxon, and the Middle English languages and means the following: Not under the control of some other person or arbitrary power, able to think without arbitrary restriction.

We shall begin by discussing what it is to be a friend. According to ancient peoples, friends were discovered in the process of a quest for a common goal or truth. Out of this discovery came mutual appreciation. As a result, friends linked up, shoulder to shoulder, and forged ahead in pursuit of their common goal or truth. Giving and receiving had no other motive than the good of the friend. Friendship enhanced the quest for a goal and, as such, friendship was a noble, unselfish virtue. This understanding of the ideal friendship allows us to compare it with the typical family and friends.

In the typical family, the "friends" expect love and affirmation. All too often, two friends come face to face, occupied with each other with the emotional needs they expect to have met by each other. There is nothing wrong with love and affirmation as long as it is not confused with friendship. People who have been through tragedies such as war, sickness, death, or divorce often experience an affinity to someone who has suffered similarly. It is as if we discover another self, another person who champions the same cause as we do and fights with equal vigor and skill. Friendship involves two or more people who suddenly discover that they see things the same way. They share the same views of things and issues.

Here is the dividing of the way for many people. Some feel that to see things the same way as others see them is to give in or give away their power. To some it means just falling in line. Many couples who fall in love do just that, they fall into it and lose their individuality, their goals, and their dreams. Consider this statement, "Unless friendship is about something, there is no friendship at all." In the family we should be friends because we all have something in common. Friends will admire another's ability to fight for a common cause and protect against evils that affect wholesome relationships.

When disaster strikes a family and splits it apart, the dilemma arises, not so much how can I be neutral being friends to both sides of the rift, but whom shall I allow to be in the seat of power? The question arises now, who will be my best friend? To whom shall I give my allegiance? There is never a balance of power in a split family. One assumes the power, and the other side is expected to fall in line.

When considering having a good friend, it is necessary to be a good friend. Consider this, if we would develop those qualities that would make a person a good friend, we would find our own company enjoyable. If so, we would never be without a friend. The most important thing when making friends is to be friendly. Who should be your best friend then? The answer is yourself. The greatest opportunity for friendship lies within ourselves. The reason for this is we must ourselves be individuals. Some of us never attain the status of being an individual. There are several reasons for this dilemma.

Firstly, it is often the result of a poor self-image that developed in early life.

Secondly, it may be as a result of one or more unresolved "skeletons in the closet." One may think that no one knows, but one knows and usually someone else knows. For sure, God knows that when we hold guilt and bitterness against someone else for our own shortcomings we are far from free. These things keep us in an emotional prison, and we are unable to be free to choose happiness, nor will we be capable of loving ourselves or others as we wish to love them.

Thirdly, sometimes we don't cultivate our individuality if we are dominated by a possessive spouse. The wife, more frequently than the husband, remains undeveloped for this reason. The role as wife and mother is all a possessive husband cares about and allows. Any sign of this wife functioning as an individual apart from the husband is met with everything from petulance to anger. The husband may apply a double standard. He may have interests, but he does not allow his wife to develop her individuality, thus splitting the family.

Fourthly, many couples, after tying the knot, think no more about wooing or loving again. Many families know little of the necessities of a happy life, emotional health, financial responsibility, or how to act toward each other. We must remember that marriage is not so much marrying the right person but being the right person.

You might rightly ask, "Is marriage putting the other person first?" Yes, marriage is a partnership, a sharing of experiences and emotions, of putting the other first. Why? As a guard against selfishness. Both marriage partners must exercise these traits or the marriage will eventually break down. Having children can draw a sharing family together or they can destroy a selfish family. You have heard the saying "love your neighbor as yourself." This quotation, this love, presupposes a healthy self-love and self-respect. We are not to love our neighbor instead of ourselves, but as ourselves. We are able to give to others only out of the fullness of our own joy. When we have a fullness of love in ourselves, it will flow to others as they ought to be loved. This is "loving your neighbor as yourself" in its true sense. In a happy and successful marriage, the partners must develop their own individuality, not living in the other's shadow. Careers are equally important for both partners. Each partner's choices must be appreciated and cherished, otherwise the marriage runs a great danger of failure.

It is important to also discuss misunderstandings. We all possess the strange tendency to misinterpret the actions of others. At some point in our lives, something we say or do will be misinterpreted by someone. There are three components to misunderstandings:

1. An action takes place. Actions are inevitable because we are dynamic beings. We realize our potential through our actions. These actions can lead to conflict through misinterpretation.

2. Evaluative perception. Even though our perception of an action may be absolutely correct, it may be very different from the actual motives of the one doing the action. Many times the meaning and purpose of an action lies deep inside the person and is inaccessible to the observer. Logic, therefore, can fail in interpreting an action.

3. Reaction misinformation. This tends to create conflicts inside and outside the family and can destroy families and marriages.

As a climax to this concept of misunderstanding, we must always seek understanding through communication. One must recognize that it is impossible to penetrate the human heart to uncover the forces that brought into existence a particular action without talking about it. What is inside is known only if the person reveals it. Sharing helps prevent conflict. Communicating with each other in friendship and sincerely desiring to understand situations and actions will allow each to choose to be closer and feel freer with each other. Talking freely of our feelings, plans, and events will bring happiness, and the family will be preserved, freedom to choose will be restored, and tensions will be reduced.

A family that communicates will feel fee to discuss dreams, hopes, plans, and fears and insecurities. A happy family is a family of friends.

Sadness and Joy

In the summer of 1961, while attending Loma Linda University in California, I had a dream. On several occasions since then I have had experiences that caused me to recall the dream. As a result, the experience remains vivid in my memory, even fifty years later, as I record it here.

My dream began as I and a group of fellow medical students were walking happily down a street that was paved with beautiful, shiny, smooth slabs of fine marble. It was a very nice day. Suddenly I found myself alone, and the marble slabs were now shattered into crushed rock under my feet. A fence stopped my progress, so I stepped aside to find myself in a room in a building that I recognized as my dwelling place at that time. Close by was a child of about twelve years of age. I recognized him as a young version of myself. I was advising the boy about choices.

Now the dream changed again, and I was outdoors in front of the dwelling. To my left side was a partially constructed building that appeared to be on the verge of collapsing unless someone intervened to fix it and save it. There were no workers present, and I was confused as to what I should do. As I stood there in dismay, a person came and sat on a nearby chair. This person appeared of great stature, wise and calming. He pointed and directed me to an area by my right side. I moved in that direction, and to my surprise, I saw the blueprint to the partially assembled building. The blueprint was lying on the ground and intact. I picked up the plan for the building, and at that moment I awakened from my dream.

Upon analyzing the dream, I learned lessons that have helped me greatly when I was in danger of losing my way. That road I trod was smooth and bright and happy. It was my experience in medical school. The sudden, drastic change happened when my brother Ronald, who was one year ahead of me, was killed in a car accident. I found myself in a real dilemma. The portion of my dream with myself as the child represented self-discipline. Self-discipline, as I understand it, is the sum total of what one has learned from parents, personal experience, faith, and hope. Such an upheaval in my life made me reevaluate everything again. I realized the partially finished building represented my partially completed course in medicine. I decided then to carry on toward my original goal—the blueprint for my life.

In reality, I had a setback, a test, a trial, but with God's guidance I overcame it and became more secure in my faith. This same dream became my guide when I met trials in the years to come. I have always interpreted that person in my dream as my personal trainer, my Savior, God. Along the way I learned that many of my decisions, even though made to the best of my ability, did not bring happiness or add joy to my life. Following these experiences I finally began asking God to help in planning my future. What a wonderful change. My decisions were more coherent, my joy increased, and I felt much more secure.

During those earlier dark days when it seemed that I had lost so very much, I knew I had something that no one could destroy. For a while I thought it was my education, but later I realized that, except for the grace of God and His guidance, I would not have had that either. What I gained was a sustaining faith and joy, knowing that the Lord was leading and blessing me.

I recall that at the age of fourteen I developed the desire to do artistic things. I carved, colored, painted, and sketched. While attending Walla Walla I took a commercial arts course. I used this knowledge as I taught the junior Sabbath School class. Many years passed after that, but I always yearned for the opportunity to paint again. Then one day while I was driving north from Burks Falls, Ontario, a sign caught my eye. I was immediately impressed to investigate it. The sign read Cabin Art Studio. I had never been in an art studio and was excited to think of the possibilities. A delightful display of paintings greeted me, and I purchased two small paintings. Before leaving I asked if they ever taught art classes. I was told that they were running a series of lessons the next week. I canceled my office appointments for the next week and entered a new chapter in life as an artist.

The art school operated between May 24 and Labor Day each summer, and I took lessons every Wednesday for the next three years. By the end of those three years, the art studio and cabin were for sale. The owner and artist teacher were moving where the owner's mother lived. The price was right, so I offered to purchase the property, and it was accepted. The art teacher quickly moved everything out so I could take possession.

Almost immediately the teacher suffered a stroke from a brain aneurysm and died. Now I was obliged to complete legal and financial matters with the owner, Anne Longfield. These circumstances drew Anne and I together, and over the next several months our eyes were opened and an affection developed that proved amazing. A year later we were married.

Looking back it seems that God gave me the desire to be artistic. That I would eventually find a person with such a similar childhood, similar tastes, and one of obvious great faith in God could only be a blessing. I felt divinely guided, and my joy is full. Anne and I cannot imagine that any other force in the universe could have been in place that could have brought us together in such a miraculous way. We thank God for leading us on this journey.

Sin and Salvation

The word sin has been in use from antiquity. In the Bible sin is the transgression of God's law, for which the penalty is death. The word sin comes from the verb "to miss." In the spiritual sense we have all missed the mark, the intended goal or target. We will all miss the mark if we do not accept God's gift of salvation.

The battle rages daily for our souls; the devil works hard to confuse us. But God has power over the source of sin and invites us to choose the great reward awaiting the faithful. We are encouraged to put on the whole armor of God, and He will do battle for us against the enemy. God supplies all the necessary pieces for the battle, and we are safe with His protection. As a soldier of God we will have good judgment, clear vision, and great strength and endurance.

Sin is likened to a festering sore that, if not healed, always leads to death. We have been assured and promised that there is a healing available, provided by our Creator. The word salvation has in it the word "salve." The healing salve is referred to as the balm of Gilead. Gilead is a region near Jordan where an evergreen tree grew in ancient days. It is of the family myrrh and resembles the Canadian balsam tree. This tree had blisters in its bark which when distilled produced a very potent healing substance. This was used in various medicines and salves.

Spiritually, the balm of Gilead is Jesus. God sent His Son as the holy ointment to heal all who desire healing from the festering sore of sin. Jesus accomplished this through His life, His words, His touch, and finally through His death and resurrection. Healing takes place over our lifetime in the process called salvation. When our healing is complete and we rest in the grave, we shall see Jesus face to face when He returns. Then we will experience true joy as we rest safely in His arms forever.

Forgiving and Forgiven

Forgiveness is expressed as a very essential instrument in understanding God's plan for our salvation. Jesus' life was the perfect example of what God will do for us when we follow His example. None of us are expected to do what Jesus did for the human race. By faith we accept the gift given us through Jesus' sacrifice. There are many facets to examine when we look further into the reasons for and the results of forgiveness. Study of this topic will result in a beautiful picture of Jesus and the hope we have for salvation in Him. Areas for consideration of this subject include what, who, how, why, when, and where.

Firstly, we must consider *what* forgiveness means. From Genesis to Revelation, forgiveness means to lift up, pardon, spare, and respect. These words include to give up resentment against or the desire to punish, or to stop being angry with, overlook, cancel, or remit a debt.

To lift up has the beautiful picture of one lifting another out of the mire of guilt and despair to a level where there is love and hope. Jesus does this for us when we follow His example, forgiving those who have wronged us. God commanded us to "love thy neighbour as thyself" (Matt. 19:19). By pardoning and respecting the person who has caused me harm, I am reflecting Jesus and His work in me for my salvation.

Who deserves forgiveness. The statement "for all have sinned, and come short of the glory of God" tells us that everyone needs forgiveness (Rom. 3:23). Recently, a pastor stated that our birth certificate registers us as sinners. No one enters into this world sinless, "no not one." Our first parents failed the test of their obedience to God, and as a result, sin entered into the human race and this world. The only way we can have hope for a life that follows Jesus' example is to learn how to forgive. Only then can we be assured of eternal life with Him. Forgive and be forgiven is the invitation to experience eternal life. This hope will create in us a life that was pure as was the life of Adam and Eve before their fall. We can be sure of our salvation because God's promises are sure.

Why should anyone even consider forgiving anyone who has caused pain and suffering? It is possible that we have been living in such close proximity to sin that we have become less sensitive to it. Unless I believe, trust, and obey my Creator and Savior, I will have no inclination to forgive anyone for anything.

Jesus knows every aspect of each and every one of our lives. He knows us far better than we know ourselves. Our trust in and obedience to God opens the way for us to appreciate His salvation and His goodness. We all need God's guidance, and He has promised to direct our ways if we ask it of Him.

While suspended on the cross, Jesus prayed, "Father, forgive them; for they know not what they do" (Luke 23:34). He forgave those who were sinning against Him.

How? Jesus said, "Come to Me, so I can come to you." Salvation is attainable by following clear and simple instructions. "Believe on the Lord Jesus Christ, and thou shalt be saved" (Acts 16:31). Believe includes trusting and obeying; trust includes faith; obedience includes following His commands.

In the New Testament, there are three commands given in addition to the Ten Commandments of Exodus 20. These three commands provide the means by which one can secure and maintain a connection with God.

1. Pray without ceasing.
2. Study to show yourself approved.
3. Tell the good news to someone.

Prayer connects us to God; study increases our understanding of God; and when we experience such a great hope for our salvation, we cannot remain silent.

When? Forgiveness must be accomplished while there is yet time. Yesterday is past, and letting the opportunity pass by one day may forever be too late. To wait for a more opportune time is a delay that may be endless. The only time to forgive is now. In the Lord's prayer, we ask to be forgiven as we forgive others. To neglect the opportunity to have our sins forgiven may mean our failure to be with Jesus through eternity. Realizing the shortness of our lifetime, we understand that this is a time-limited offer.

Where? Forgiveness occurs at the foot of the cross, a symbolic cross. The cross is a symbol of Jesus' sacrifice, His humility, and His victory over sin. When we kneel in prayer, it is a symbol of our kneeling at the foot of the cross. By forgiving others and asking for personal forgiveness, we have faith that we are forgiven. All sins must be confessed to God because only God can forgive sin. It is good for the forgiven to know that the burden of guilt has been lifted and the debt canceled.

A most important conclusion to forgiveness is that of forgiving ourselves. Having asked God, the only one who can forgive us our sins, and believing that we have been forgiven, we must forgive ourselves. This is evidence that the sin has been erased from our record. A person said that even though God had forgiven the sin, he could not forgive himself. Such a condition means that the person is still carrying the sin as though it was not forgiven. The person has not accepted God's gift of forgiveness. Forgiveness is complete when we have the faith to believe that we are forgiven.

Time Travel

This thought could have had several titles. It could have been called "What I Learned About Life" or "My Philosophy of Life." It was in college that my teacher gave us an assignment in composition and grammar class and asked us to write a short essay on "My Philosophy of Life." To begin with, I didn't know what philosophy really meant, so I looked up the meaning in the dictionary and other reference books.

I finally felt as if I knew what I was to write about. I needed to discuss where I had come from, what I was doing, and where I was going. Where I came from meant reviewing my life so far. I had memories of my parents, my siblings, and the world around me and the influences they had on me. What I was doing was easier because I was in school. Where I was going was based on my plans for the future, my hopes, intentions, and my parents' hopes for me. Getting ahead would depend on the attention I would give it and my determination to get there.

In composing my story, I contemplated how far back in time and history I should go. I could read about my ancestors in history books. Beyond the history books, I could go further into the past by referring to the oldest book, the Bible. On opening that book, I read the first four words—"In the beginning, God...."

It was a revelation to me that God was there in the beginning, and the beginning is beyond my imagination. One thing I was sure of was that one can always be sure of time. One second is always one second long, and there are sixty seconds in one minute.

My third part of the essay was a little easier. My future was my plans and my hopes for life ahead. Suddenly I realized I was a "time traveler," for in my mind, I could go back in time for a very long distance, and I could go into the future by looking forward to eternity. By this time I was curious to find if the Bible referred to these entities of time. I found what seemed to be a possible reference. It was the passage that spoke of faith, hope, and charity (1 Cor. 13:13).

Faith is based on what we have learned to be true and dependable from our past. Hope is what we believe for our future based on our studies and the faithfulness of those who have given us enlightenment. Charity, another word for love, is something we can appreciate only in the present. The present is the only time we can experience love, the only time we can express our love, the only time we can make decisions. Thus it is the most important of the three.

This was the essence of my little dissertation on my philosophy of life.

Time of Trouble

John 14:1 says, "Let not your heart be troubled: ye believe in God, believe also in me." Jesus has our happiness in His best interest. He said that whatever we ask in His name it will be done. "In His name" precludes having a loving relationship with Him and a willingness to obey Him. Jesus said, "If ye love me, keep my commandments" (John 14:15). Jesus said that we will find Him if we search for Him with all our heart and soul and mind. Those are the spiritual, physical, and intellectual aspects of our beings.

With this in mind, Jesus implored us to not allow ourselves to become troubled. Troubled has the connotation of confusion, stirred up, seeing only the negative, degeneration, and calamities. All of these feelings can cause discouragement. Jesus invites us to trust Him and have faith in Him. When we obey His commandments, we exhibit our connection to and faith in Him. With this loving relationship, we are able to have a joyful outlook for the future, no matter what the present brings to us.

Many people are fearful of what they perceive as the future time of trouble. For many who do not have faith in Jesus, the time of trouble is all around and never ends. They only see the natural disasters, the crime, and the wars, and they wonder when their time will come to an end. By being prepared we will not be afraid. Our preparation is to develop that loving relationship with our Creator.

For example, when we walk outdoors in the darkness of night, we are careful with each step we take in order not to stumble or fall along the way. So it is when we walk in the uncertainty of this sinful world. We must watch for all the guideposts and signs along the way and be aware of Jesus' directions as we journey toward heaven. Jesus assures us of salvation and a joy that is far superior to any sadness we experience here.

If we choose Him as our Creator, Sustainer, and Savior, we have the assurance of eternity with Jesus, and it is near, "even at the doors" (Matt. 24:33). This is the time to make sure our anchor holds to the Rock and that Rock is Jesus.

The Wise Men

The wise men from the East were not Magi. The root word of magician is magi, and these men were not using magic when they followed the star. These men were of those who had studied the prophesies and especially were drawn to the prophesies of Jeremiah. They studied, believed, and acted on their faith when God impressed them to follow the star. They knew by the prophecies that a King of the Jews was to be born at that appointed time, and they traveled west to find Him.

These men were full of knowledge and understanding, and they recognized the star as a sign from heaven. Depending on the mode of travel they had at their disposal, it may have taken up to two months to arrive at their destination. On their way they came to Jerusalem and inquired of Herod if he knew where the babe was located. Herod learned from the Jews that Bethlehem was the most likely place. The wise men followed the star to Bethlehem and found the babe, not in the manger, but in a house with His family.

At least three wise men arrived. There may be several interpretations to this scene. The small number could represent the remnant of believers, or the Trinity (the Father, Son, and Holy Spirit). Looking at the gifts will clarify this to some extent.

The choice of the gifts was not an accident. They were chosen for their special purpose. Gold, in this context, is to furnish what is needed, as in a charitable act toward someone. Frankincense, as seen in the tabernacle in the wilderness, represents prayer, communion with God, a sweet-smelling fragrance. Myrrh, an ointment of great value, is a healing salve for everyone who believes. It represented completeness, love for the brethren, giving as to a friend. These gifts were offered to Jesus not for their monetary value only but for what the gifts represented. God supplies all our needs, He invites us to come directly to Him for help, and He will heal all our wounds and infirmities. As with the wise men, if we believe in and follow God all things are possible.

Jesus grew in stature and in the knowledge of God. Jesus is the embodiment of these gifts, the source of all things good, our way to God, and through His loving sacrifice He made it possible for us to live forever. The wise men represent all those who believe and who faithfully follow Him.

Thoughts From Job

In the record of Job, we find that Job lost his possessions and his children. His wife's security was threatened if her husband died at this time. Job was suffering intolerably and was not sure he would survive. All those close to him thought, as well, that he might die. With this in mind, we see that his wife was deeply concerned about Job's state of mind. Joy and sadness were thought of differently in those days.

The prosperity, uprightness, and innocence of a person were considered gifts from God. In contrast, suffering and loss of material things were considered a result of sin; therefore, Job must have sinned.

Job held to his integrity, claiming to be innocent of even unknown sin. But he did not claim to understand God's actions or judgment, and he could not understand why God was allowing him to suffer so. Job reasoned that if God let an innocent person suffer so severely, why would He have allowed him to be born. If he had not been born, he would have avoided all this suffering.

Job realized that he had no right to question God's treatment of him. Job did not allow any negative thoughts of God to enter his mind. He made small speeches and a dissertation on why we should hold to our faith in God whether accused of evil, sin, or just being abused for no reason. In Job's case Satan had claimed that Job would be treasonous toward God if he was made to suffer. God allowed Satan to maltreat Job, knowing Job's heart and his faithfulness.

In Job 2:9, Job's wife made a simple statement that has deep meaning; she said, "Curse God, and die." Under those circumstances, if Job were to give up and die, God would lose, and Job would be a curse to God. While attempting to find where he may have sinned, Job said that he had not imprecated anyone, that is, he had not made an oath against anyone, used God's name profanely, or wished evil against anyone.

After Job prays for deliverance. God calls a halt to the satanic attack on him, and Job was greatly blessed for his faith. His life and possessions were restored and his integrity remained intact.

Our Lord's Prayer

The prayer Jesus taught us has many messages (Matt. 6:9–13). "Our Father" acknowledges that we are His children. As His children, we have the privilege to call Him Father. "Who art" tells us that God exists in the present and has been in the past and will be in the future. "In heaven" refers to God's home, a place of eternal joy and the place all believers will go to upon His second coming.

"Hallowed be thy name" recognizes that only God is holy, the source of all things good and merciful and gracious. "Thy kingdom come" reveals our desire to be with Jesus in heaven. "Thy will be done" refers to the fact that we ask God to do His will because we realize that His will is the good path on which He is leading us.

"Give us this day our daily bread" recognizes God as the source of our sustenance, the Bread of Life. We ask for a daily allotment so we can serve Him spiritually, emotionally, and physically.

"Forgive us our sins" acknowledges that only God can forgive sin. Jesus instructed us to forgive those who treat us poorly; thus, we follow His example and show compassion to sinners as He does.

"Lead us" has great meaning. By our submission to and trust in God, we have faith to ask Him to take us by the hand and lead us in the safe paths through this life. "Not into temptation, but deliver us from evil" is a request to be protected and delivered from the wiles of the evil one. Temptation is always present, but overcoming temptation is always possible through Jesus.

"For thine is the kingdom and the power and the glory forever" recognizes the qualities of God and the salvation that is offered through Him. Finally, we ask God to carry out His will in us as we submit totally to Him. This is the "Amen."

Jealousy

In Exodus 20:5 God states that He is a jealous God. For many years I believed that jealousy was a negative trait and was to be avoided; then I wondered how a loving God could be jealous. I know that God is love, merciful, true, and always uplifting. I realized that I needed to study the meaning of that word. In the search that followed, I found both a positive and a negative meaning for jealousy.

In the second commandment, I found both the positive and the negative aspects of the word. It is explained right there in plain sight. To put anything or anyone above God is to sin against God. The effects of sin are so serious that, even when forgiven, its effects remain in the family for three to four generations. A child's greatest teachers are its parents, and when they are dedicated to God, the effects of sin are gradually overcome.

The second meaning of the word jealousy speaks of a warm relationship with our Creator, our heavenly Father. When it is "our will" to follow God's plan for salvation, He gives us grace and shows mercy. Our relationship is "warm" with Him.

When we experience abuse or neglect, it is a normal human reaction to feel a measure of anger and a desire for retaliation. But God teaches us to replace anger with forgiveness. We are to love our neighbors as ourselves, meaning, since we are all sinners, we must not judge anyone's sin as worse than our own. No matter what the sin is, the penalty is always the same. Forgiveness is God's remedy for anger and is Jesus' example for us to follow, thus allowing every human being the choice of repentance and salvation. Through forgiveness we lift up our neighbors and show them Jesus' love.

Through forgiveness of an unkind act, the beginning of a new and wonderful relationship with our neighbor and with God can occur. Jesus taught us that it is our privilege and duty to practice what He did. This is "jealous for" not "jealous of." Our God is jealous for His children. Let us choose this day to follow Jesus' example and be a child of God.

Loaves and Fishes

The feeding of the five thousand reveals a sad story with a beautiful ending. There are several messages to consider, both symbolic and real. The news of John the Baptist's execution had just been released to the people of the region, and when Jesus heard of his death, He was saddened. Jesus left the area and took a boat to a secluded area in order to grieve. The people found out where He was going and followed Him on foot.

When Jesus arrived at His destination, He saw a huge number of people gathering there. They numbered five thousand men plus women and children. Jesus immediately had compassion on them and healed the sick. He also took time to feed them spiritually until they were filled with His blessings. Evening drew near, and it was obvious that these dear people were now physically hungry. The disciples asked if they should send the multitude away so they might go and find food. Jesus told them that it was not necessary but that they should feed them. That is when they found a little boy with five loaves and two fishes, which they brought to Jesus at His request. The number seven is a perfect number and symbolizes that however little we have to offer, Jesus counts it as a perfect gift. He has promised to bless us when we bring our gifts to Him.

In this place Jesus blessed the gift so abundantly that the few morsels fed the whole multitude. They were a happy and fulfilled multitude of followers. They believed and received physical healing and were made whole spiritually.

So what will He do when we come to Him with our spiritual and physical needs? He will bless us abundantly.

Water of Life

Water is necessary for life, but it must be clear, fresh, and pure to benefit us. If water is left unattended and unused, it can become polluted, stale, and even disease bearing. In our bodies, water is necessary for cleansing, digestion, hydration, and elimination of waste.

Spiritually, we require the Water of Life for cleansing and nourishment of the soul and for discernment. The Water of Life is always available and flows freely to all who seek God. If a constant flow of spiritual water is not kept intact, one is susceptible to many dangers. The connection to the Water of Life is sustained by the study of God's Word and prayer. Neglect of study and prayer leads to a failure of the system, and though almost unnoticeable at first, it is surely fatal to the soul. When one becomes aware of the poor condition of the "water" supply, one must go to the Creator in order to fix the problem. Repentance and conversion are the results of turning to Christ.

Prevention is always superior to repair, so it is necessary to keep the Water of Life always present through study and prayer. Constant guidance is necessary for success in our lives, and we have only to ask our Creator to walk by our side daily in order to succeed.

Work and Success

Work is defined as mental or physical effort exerted to do something. In an abbreviated form, work is purposeful activity. A child works diligently to walk and talk. As one matures, one finds it necessary to exert effort in order to succeed in one's intention for life. Young people are told they can do anything they wish to do. Wisdom prevails when a person narrows all those choices to a few favorite ones. As young people mature they find that one challenge is often enough. In mid life one realizes that one objective in life is plenty and one makes efforts to accomplish the greater objectives with the best use of their energy.

Unfortunately, there are some who feel that success is measured in wealth and possessions. They work harder and harder, believing that they are being a good provider and a good partner and parent. Their goal is never reached, so they work even harder. This condition is known as being a workaholic. As a result of this work ethic, relationships suffer and friends become scarce.

Somewhere in the game of life one must balance the expenditure of energy between the physical, the intellectual, and the spiritual. To have peace of mind and success in one's family and with one's friends we must focus on the spiritual things of this world.

Babel Undone

In the January 2010 issue of *Adventist World*, I read an article titled "Babel Undone." I became excited when I considered the meanings one could glean from those words. I read about the people who lived after the great flood of Genesis and how they were determined to take care of themselves. They set about to build a tower so high that no flood would be able to reach the top, just in case God decided to destroy the earth again. They were determined to save themselves.

God loved these people, and although He could have destroyed them, He did the loving thing and just made it impossible for them to accomplish their task. God confused their languages so that the people were forced to move away from each other to different parts of the world. Even at that time there were followers of God who taught their families about the only true way to be saved.

As a result of the confusion of languages at the tower of Babel, we have many languages around the world. Gradually, God has allowed us to learn foreign languages, thus decreasing the total confusion of Genesis. A complete reversal of Babel is not only possible but expected, and it will be accomplished by God at Jesus' second coming. All God's chosen will be caught up to Him and our new life will include a new language. This language will be the real language of heaven, the language of love. I am excited to realize that I will know a new language without having to take a single lesson. What a wonderful God we serve.

The First Seventh-day Adventists

The Genesis record of Creation ends with the seventh day being set aside as a day of rest by the Creator. The day was blessed and has been kept by His followers throughout history as a memorial of Creation. Throughout the six thousand years that have passed since God hallowed that special day, there has always been a group of believers who have kept the Sabbath as God's holy day. Sabbath literally means rest.

In the time of Noah, very few people kept God's word, and it was God's decision to use this little group, a remnant, to restart the human race. Since that time there has been a group of followers, sometimes small, but always faithful and growing in numbers. The seventh-day Sabbath has always been recognized as God's holy day, and it remains today as a mark of faith in God's Word.

God asked Moses to make a record of early history. In the book of Exodus, Moses recorded the events surrounding the presentation of the Ten Commandments to the children of Israel while they lived in the wilderness. The fourth commandment, which addresses the Sabbath, begins with the word remember. God knew that this commandment would be the most abused and forgotten of the ten.

But God has always had a people who have followed the fourth commandment. If you think about it, the disciples were Sabbatarians. They followed Jesus' example and worshiped on the seventh day of the week, the Sabbath. Upon Jesus' resurrection, He instructed His disciples that He would return one day to take all of His followers home with Him to heaven. The disciples recognized Jesus as the Son of God and believed in the second advent of Christ. The disciples were, therefore, the very first Seventh-day Adventists.

Of course, approximately 1850 years after the first advent a small group of believers officially adopted the name Seventh-day Adventist. Since the mid-1850s that little group of believers has grown to millions who eagerly await Jesus' second coming. Let us continue to remember the Sabbath day to keep it holy.

Joyful End-Times

There appears to be considerable anxiety in the anticipation of the end-times. Biblically, the period referred to is the time between the first and second coming of Jesus. To the Christian, it is a matter of being prepared for the transition from life to death. When one considers the time humanity has spent on earth compared to eternity, one would logically conclude that we have been living in what can be referred to as the beginning. The end of this beginning appears to be what causes some folks to be anxious. But we must remember that in order to begin eternity, there must be an end.

There are only two ways a Christian can enter into the new life. The first is to sleep in Jesus, which we know as death, followed by the resurrection to life everlasting. The second way to reach eternity is by translation at Jesus' second coming. If we are still alive when Jesus returns, we will be changed in the blink of an eye. There is no appreciation of time when we are asleep in Jesus. So don't be afraid of the dark; after the night comes the morning, bright and glorious.

The end of this "beginning" is a period of grace given to us by God so we can choose Him and prepare to meet Him. This should not be a fearful time but an opportunity to choose our most wonderful future and prepare for it. Only those who have not found Jesus and have not developed a loving faith in Him should be fearful for their future.

For the believer, it is a time filled with hope, reassurance, and acceptance of His promises for a closer walk with our Creator. Armed with the armor of God and practicing the fruits of the Spirit, many will face trials, tests, and pain, but they will always feel the love of God and experience peace in their souls. But we can love life, for it is our time and opportunity to choose our future and to experience increasing joy as we witness for Christ.

Knowing that a loving God is constantly watching and caring for one's soul is most reassuring and promotes great faith and healing. Without such a great sacrifice by God, we would have no hope, but He has made it possible through His death that everyone has an equal opportunity to be with Him.

After we have confessed that we have sinned against God, humanity, and ourselves and have received forgiveness, there remains three guidelines to enhance our daily growth. As I have mentioned before, they are pray without ceasing, study to show yourself approved, and tell someone the good news. With this preparation one cannot possibly fail to draw souls to Christ.

We invite you to view the complete
selection of titles we publish at:

www.TEACHServices.com

Scan with your mobile
device to go directly
to our website.

Please write or email us your praises, reactions, or
thoughts about this or any other book we publish at:

TEACH Services, Inc.

P U B L I S H I N G

www.TEACHServices.com

P.O. Box 954
Ringgold, GA 30736

info@TEACHServices.com

TEACH Services, Inc., titles may be purchased in bulk for
educational, business, fund-raising, or sales promotional
use.
For information, please e-mail:

BulkSales@TEACHServices.com

Finally, if you are interested in seeing
your own book in print, please contact us at

publishing@TEACHServices.com

We would be happy to review your manuscript for free.